Games Around the World

Chess

by Dana Meachen Rau

Content Adviser: Glenn Petersen, United States Chess Federation

Reading Adviser: Rosemary G. Palmer, Ph.D., Department of Literacy,
College of Education, Boise State University

COMPASS POINT BOOKS MINNEAPOLIS, MINNESOTA

Compass Point Books
3109 West 50th Street, #115
Minneapolis, MN 55410

Visit Compass Point Books on the Internet at *www.compasspointbooks.com*
or e-mail your request to *custserv@compasspointbooks.com*

Photographs ©: Gary Sundermeyer, cover, 10, 11, 15; Stockbyte, 2 (all), 8 (all);
Stock Montage, 4; Corbis, 5; Giraudon/Art Resource, N.Y., 6; Werner Forman/Art Resource,
N.Y., 7; John Gichigi/Allsport by Getty Images, 9; David Forman/Eye Ubiquitous/Corbis, 12;
Ronnie Kaufman/Corbis, 13; Chris Lowe/Index Stock Imagery, 24, 27.

Creative Director: Terri Foley
Managing Editor: Catherine Neitge
Editor: Jennifer VanVoorst
Photo Researcher: Svetlana Zhurkina
Designer/Page production: Bradfordesign, Inc./Jaime Martens
Illustrator: Jaime Martens
Educational Consultant: Diane Smolinski

Library of Congress Cataloging-in-Publication Data
Rau, Dana Meachen, 1971–
   Chess / by Dana Meachen Rau.
      v. cm. — (Games around the world)
   Includes bibliographical references (p.   ) and index.
   Contents: Battle on a board—The history of chess—Chess basics—
   The board—Moving the pieces—Check and checkmate—
   Special moves and rules—How a game ends—Bringing people together.
   ISBN 0-7565-0674-3 (hardcover)
      1. Chess—Juvenile literature. [1. Chess.] I. Title. II. Series.
GV1446.R38 2005
794.1—dc22   2003024093

Table of Contents

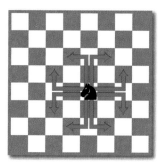

NOTE: *In this book, words that are defined in the glossary are in* **bold** *the first time they appear in the text.*

Battle on a Board

Imagine a battle long ago. A king is hiding in his castle. His lovely queen and the bishops of his church fight against the enemy to keep him safe. The knights ride in on their horses. The men of the army march forward. They are sure to win against the enemy and save their king.

▲ A girl studies the chess board.

But the enemy's army is strong, too. Soon the queen is captured. Then a knight is taken. The king is no longer safe. The enemy reaches the king, and the war is over.

This adventure is not just a story that takes place long ago in a faraway land. It is a game you can play right here and now. It is a game called chess.

◄ The battle that takes place on a chess board is much like a real-life battle of long ago.

The History of Chess

People all over the world have been playing chess for more than 1,000 years. People in India first played a game like chess as early as the year 500. They called their game *chaturanga.* A similar game was also played in China. It was called *hsiang chi.*

The game spread from India to Persia, known today as Iran. When the Arabs conquered Persia, they learned how to play chess, and the game became popular throughout the Arab world.

▲ Chess has been popular in India for many years.

People in Europe learned about chess from trading goods and ideas with the Arabs. By the early 11th century, chess was popular in Europe. However, only wealthy people played, and chess became known as "the game of kings."

◄ *Only wealthy people played chess in 14th-century France.*

Since the 1500s, when a few changes were made to the rules and the pieces, the game of chess has stayed the same. One thing, however, has changed. Today, all types of people play chess, not just the rich.

As chess became more popular, players didn't just want to play in their homes with friends. They wanted to play against others all over the world. In 1851, the first international chess tournament was held. It took place in London, England.

Today, there are tournaments for both adults and children. Some children start playing—and even competing—as young as 4 years old. Chess brings together people from hundreds of different countries to battle on a board.

▲ A queen from a chess set of long ago

▲ A king from a chess set of long ago

Players of all ages compete in chess tournaments. ▶

Chess Basics

Chess is a game for two players. The person you are playing against is called your **opponent.** The point of the game is to capture your opponent's king. At the same time, your opponent is trying to capture your king. So you must do two things at once: keep your king safe, and attack your opponent's king in such a way that there is no escape. The pieces used in chess are called **chessmen.** You have 16 chessmen in all. The pieces in order of their importance are: one king, one queen, two rooks (or castles), two knights, two bishops, and eight pawns.

king **queen** **rook** **knight** **bishop** **pawn**

One army of chessmen is white, and the other is black. Even when the colors on the board are different, the lighter color is called white and the darker one black. White always makes the first move. Next goes black. Then each side takes turns, moving only one piece at a time with each turn.

While your object is to capture your opponent's king, you may also capture your opponent's other chessmen. You capture a piece by landing on the square it is on. Then you take the piece off the board and replace it with your piece that landed there.

king   **queen**   **rook**   **knight**   **bishop**   **pawn**

There is a lot to think about during a chess game. You have to think about which of your chessmen to move. You also have to think about what your opponent's next move might be. You have to think about keeping your king safe. You have to think about which of your opponent's pieces you want to attack. Many players think many moves ahead. There is a lot of thinking going on!

▲ *Players watch their boards carefully to decide their next move.*

Young people and old people can compete against each other in chess. ▶

The Board

A chess board is the same kind of board that you might use to play checkers. It is made up of 64 squares—32 white and 32 black. There are eight spaces across and eight spaces down. The rows side to side are called **ranks.** The rows up and down are called **files.** The slanted rows of the same color are called **diagonals.**

To play chess, you first need to set up the board. Begin by making sure a white square is in the right corner nearest you. (The same will be true of your opponent.) It helps to think of the phrase "white at the right" when you set up the board.

14

▲ Ranks, files, and diagonals

▲ The chess board set up to begin a game

On your first rank, the one closest to you, start from each side and place a rook in each corner. Next to them place the knights, and then the bishops. The king and queen go in the two remaining center spaces. The queen always goes on the square of her own color, so the white queen always sits on a white space, and the black queen on a black space. The king goes in the last open space.

On the second rank, line up all of your pawns. Your opponent sets up his or her side in the same way.

Now you are ready to learn how each piece can move.

king **queen** **rook** **knight** **bishop** **pawn**

Moving the Pieces

Each piece must move on the board in a certain way.

PAWNS can only move forward, and only one space at a time. (On its first move, however, a pawn can move forward two spaces.) Though pawns move forward, they capture other pieces in a diagonal direction. A piece diagonally to the left or right of a pawn is in big trouble. Pawns are often thought of as unimportant, but they sometimes surprise other pieces and capture them easily.

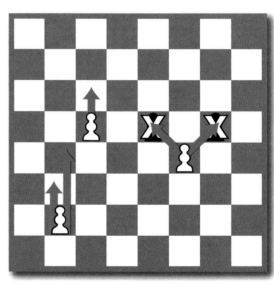

▲ *A pawn moves forward one space at a time. On its first move, however, it can move forward two spaces. It captures pieces diagonal to it.*

BISHOPS move diagonally on the board. They can move as many spaces as they want, as long as no chessmen block their way. This also means that bishops always stay on the same color squares throughout the whole game.

▲ *Bishops move diagonally on the board.*

KNIGHTS move in an L-shaped pattern. On ranks and files, they can move ahead two spaces and across one. Knights are the only pieces that can jump over other pieces, just as a horse can jump.

▲ *Knights move in an L-shaped pattern.* **17**

ROOKS move in ranks and files. They may move as many spaces as they can, as long as no chess-men block their path. Rooks are great at protecting a king. They march up and down and back and forth, ready to capture any piece that might come near.

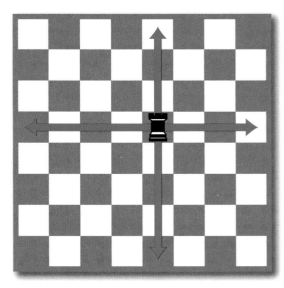

▲ *Rooks move in ranks and files.*

THE QUEEN can move across ranks, files, and diagonals in any direction as long as no piece blocks her way. Because she can move so many different ways, the queen is the most powerful piece on the board.

▲ *The queen moves along ranks, files, and diagonals.*

THE KING can move in any direction, like the queen. However, he can only move one square at a time. Sometimes during a game, the king may just stay in the first rank and not move at all. Also, a king can never move next to another king.

▲ *The king moves one square at a time in any direction.*

Tips:

- Move your knights off the back rank before you move your bishops.
- Castle early (see page 23), and move your rooks onto files where there are no pawns.
- Try not to move the same piece twice until you have moved your knights and bishops off the back rank.

Check and Checkmate

While playing, your opponent might put your king in **check**.
This means that the king can be captured on your opponent's
next move. Check is like a warning for the king to protect himself.
   If your king is in check, it forces you to make him safe again.

You can do this one of three ways:

   1.   You can move the king to a
        safe square.

   2.   You can block the check with
        one of your other chessmen.

▲ *The white queen has the black king in check,
but there are three ways he can be made safe.*

3. You can capture your opponent's piece that is attacking the king.

▲ The white king has been checkmated by the black queen. It is white's turn to move, and the white king cannot move to any safe square.

You may not be able to do any of these things. Then your opponent will call out **"checkmate."** This means that there is nothing you can do to save your king, and the game is over.

The word *chess* comes from the ancient Persian word *shah*, which means "king." *Checkmate* comes from *shah mat*—"the king is dead" in ancient Persian.

Special Moves and Rules

There are a few additional special moves and rules to keep in mind as you play:

En passant: This is a French term that means "in passing." If an opponent's pawn moves two squares on its first move and lands beside your pawn, you may take it. Then your pawn moves forward a square diagonally.

▲ 1. The black pawn moves forward two squares on its first move.

▲ 2. The black pawn now sits beside the white pawn.

▲ 3. The white pawn captures the black pawn and moves forward a square diagonally.

Castling: If your king seems to be in danger, you may want to make a move called castling. Four things must be true to make this move. First, the king and rook cannot have moved from their original squares. Second, the spaces between your king and one of your rooks have to be clear. Third, the king can't be in check. Finally, as the king moves to this new position, he cannot move through a position that would put him in check. To castle, you move your king two spaces toward the rook. Then the rook jumps over the king and sits in the space on the king's other side. You can only castle once in a game.

▲ *To castle, move the king two spaces toward the rook. Then jump the rook over the king to sit next to the king on the other side.*

A pawn reaches the end: Sometimes one or more of your pawns reaches the other end of the board without being captured. If it does, you can turn your pawn into any other piece you want. Players usually turn this pawn into a queen, since queens can move the most freely around the board.

Touching: You have to be careful of what you touch on a chess board. Once you touch one of your chessmen, you have to move it. If you touch one of your opponent's pieces, you have to capture it if you can.

▲ *Moving the king*

24

How a Game Ends

You win the game if you have checkmated your opponent's king. However, there are other ways that a game can end.

A game might be a **draw.** This happens when the players don't have enough chessmen on the board to checkmate the kings. A draw can also be reached by agreement between the players.

A game might end in **stalemate,** another type of draw. It happens when neither you nor your opponent can make any legal moves.

▲ *A draw: there are not enough pieces to checkmate.*

▲ *A stalemate: it is black's turn to move, but black has no legal moves.*

25

Bringing People Together

Now that you know the rules, you are ready to play. Because the game of chess requires so much thinking, it takes a lot of practice. From the first move to the last, every game will be different.

Chess is a great way to spend time with a friend or family member. Before the Internet, some people played "postal chess" and exchanged moves through the mail. Today, many people play chess on the computer.

Some people join chess clubs. Some play more than one game at a time. There are international tournaments with players from many countries. It doesn't matter what language players speak. Chess is a game that brings the world together.

Chess is a great way to spend time with a friend or family member. ▶

Glossary

check—when your king can be captured on your opponent's next move

checkmate—when your king is attacked and cannot escape

chessmen—the chess pieces; also known as pieces and pawns

diagonals—the slanted rows of the same color on a chess board

draw—the end of a game that does not result in checkmate

files—the rows up and down on a chess board

opponent—the person you are playing against

ranks—the rows side to side on a chess board

stalemate—the end of a game in which one player has no legal moves

Did You Know?

- The Vikings played with chess sets on their ships. The pieces had pegs in the bottom that fit into squares with holes to keep them steady on the choppy seas.

- Bobby Fischer was the youngest player to win the United States Championship. In 1958, he won when he was only 14 years old.

- Through a special code of numbers and letters, each move made in a game can be recorded. This is called chess notation. Because of chess notation, we can look at games played hundreds of years ago and see how the players moved.

- Germans call the knight a *springer*. This is because it can "spring," or jump, over other pieces on the board.

- Garry Kasparov, from Russia, is considered by many to be the best player in the world.

- U.S. scientists developed a computer to try to beat the greatest chess players. In 1997, this computer, called Deep Blue, beat Garry Kasparov. Kasparov was very upset.

- The pieces in the ancient Chinese game *hsiang chi* included elephants and chariots.

- The longest tournament chess game was played in 1989. It lasted more than 20 hours.

- Some players play "blindfolded" chess against opponents who use real sets. They picture the board in their minds and never see the pieces moving on the real board.

- Some players play a game of "speed chess" called blitz chess. Each player gets five minutes in which to make all of his or her moves.

Want to Know More?

At the Library

Cardo, Horacio. *The Story of Chess.* New York: Abbeville Press, 1998.
Harper, Piers. *Checkmate at Chess City.* Cambridge, Mass.: Candlewick Press, 2000.
King, Daniel. *Chess: From First Moves to Checkmate.* New York: Kingfisher, 2000.

On the Web

For more information on chess, use FactHound
to track down Web sites related to this book.

1. Go to *www.facthound.com*
2. Type in a search word related to this book
   or this book ID: 0756506743
3. Click on the *Fetch It* button.

Your trusty FactHound will fetch the best Web sites for you!

On the Road

U.S. Chess Center
1501 M St. N.W.
Washington, D.C. 20005
202/857-4922
To take lessons, participate in tournaments, or even attend
summer chess camp

**World Chess Hall of Fame and
Sidney Samole Chess Museum**
13755 S.W. 119th Ave.
Miami, FL 33186
786/242-HALL (4255)
info@chessmuseum.org
To see important memorabilia of the history of chess
and even play with a life-size set

Index

About the Author

Dana Meachen Rau is an author, editor, and illustrator.
A graduate of Trinity College in Hartford, Connecticut,
she has written more than 90 books for children, including
nonfiction, biographies, early readers, and historical fiction.
Ms. Rau loves to play games. She plays chess in Burlington,
Connecticut, with her husband, Chris, and children,
Charlie and Allison.